LESSONS FROM A DYING SAVIOR

Dr. Ephraim "Pop" Williams,

Thank you for sowing into my life and ministry. Thank you for adopting me as a spiritual son. Your love, trust, faith, encouragement and support mean more than words can express. I pray God's richest blessings upon your life.

"Live the Lessons!"

— Matthew 28:19, 20 —

Your Son,

Clay

9 July 2006

LESSONS FROM A DYING SAVIOR

By

Claybon Lea, Jr., D.Min.

Relevant Publishing
Creative Publishing for Creative Minds.

Published by
Relevant Publishing
2275 Murfreesboro Pike, Suite 100
Nashville, TN 37217
615-366-3211

Unless otherwise noted, all scripture
quotations are taken from the HOLY
BIBLE, NEW INTERNATIONAL
VERSION®. NIV®. Copyright ©1973,
1978, 1984 by International Bible Society.
Used by permission of Zondervan. All
rights reserved.

ISBN 0-9764174-2-1
Photography: Mr. K's Mobil Photos

Table of Contents

Foreword

At last! God is to be praised and I am elated that finally the Christian community has a timely, insightful, thoughtful, and provocative document that returns us to the ultimate symbol of our Christian faith– the cross of Jesus the Christ! Have you noticed, as I have, the weekly proclamation of many who purport to be Christian preachers <u>and</u> never mention the cross? Are you conscious of the many contemporary sanctuaries built in the name of the Savior and, yet, the cross – our undeniable symbol – is nowhere to be found? It is almost as if the cross of the Christ has become an embarrassment to those who claim redemption through the Nazarene.

Dr. Claybon Lea, Jr. has dipped his bucket in an old well and secured for the community of faith fresh and invigorating water. He has allowed the Holy Spirit to prayerfully and skillfully navigate him through those time honored verses in New Testament writ that articulate the seven sayings of our Lord from Calvary's cross. In so many ways the seven sayings of our Lord Jesus Christ from the cross have almost become irrelevant and nominal, lifted only annually on Good Friday when scant and quick attention are attached to them in a worship experience designed for approximately three hours. Dr. Lea forces us to look anew and afresh at the seven sayings and their life changing and challenging appeal. From exegesis to insight to practical application, Dr. Lea takes us on a journey that is needful and necessary for what Harry Emerson Fosdick calls "the living of these days."

Immerse yourself in these leaves of passion and inspiration and be encouraged from the pen and heart of this pastor-preacher-prophet.

Dr. Charles E. Booth
Pastor of Mt. Olivet Baptist Church
Columbus, Ohio

Dedication

This book is dedicated to

my late father, Reverend Claybon Lea, Sr.,
my living mother, Carol Vinson Lea

&

my beloved Pastor and mentor, the late Dr.
William Augustus Jones, Jr.

I owe my foundational acquaintance with
and articulation of, the Savior to these
sincere and substantive saints of God.

Acknowledgments

First and foremost, I thank God for my salvation through Jesus the Christ. Moreover, God be praised for this blessed opportunity to share insights and illuminations with the world. Secondly, to my wife and children ("The Leavites"), thank you for loving me and letting me lead you. Thirdly, to Katie Sherman and my entire editing team, thank you for your labor of love. Also, to my friend, Bishop Joseph W. Walker, III, thanks for everything. You and Denise Foxworth made it happen! In addition, a special thanks goes out to my special friends for their prayers, encouragement and willingness to hold me accountable. Finally, I thank God for the Mt. Calvary Church where I am privileged to teach and preach the lessons of our Savior weekly.

God be Praised!

Inspiration

I am the cross
I am the symbol of the vicarious suffering of Jesus
Christ.
I am the emblem of God's costly love in seeking to
save humanity from sin.
I am Christ's final acceptance of and submission to
the will of the Father.
I am a demonstration of the utter iniquity and
moral perversity of sin.
I am the burden of sorrow and suffering which sin
places upon those who share Christ's passion to rid
the world of sin.
I show how ethically blind religious fanatics can be.
I am the God-given assurance of the ultimate
victory over sin.
I am God's instrument to provide comfort,
resignation and fortitude for those who are the
victims of aggressive evil.
I demonstrate the possibility of man's willingness to
give his life for the welfare of others.
I give drawing power to the Gospel.
I am the utmost effort of evil to frustrate God's
plan of redemption.
I justify the attitudes of gratitude, loyal devotion
and worship toward Jesus Christ.
I am the turning point in the religious history of
humanity.

I provide a way by which those who have been guilty
of wrongdoing may establish fellowship with the
God of righteousness.
I am the cross.

(Norman E. Richardson)

Prologue

What makes the cross so important? What makes the cross so central to Christianity? Why is it the focus of our faith? Why does it define our identity?

The cross is everything to us because as He died on it, Jesus taught us the central principles of our faith.

Our Lord and Savior did more than just surrender His back to the crushing blows of a cat o' nine tails. He did more than just surrender His head to a crown of thorns and His side to the piercing thrust of a spear. He did more than just surrender His hands and feet to spikes and His weakening body to the law of gravity.

Jesus did far more than just die on that cross.

While suffering in agonizing pain and paying the price for our redemption, Jesus taught us lessons for *living*. By turning Calvary into a classroom, He proved that He was the ultimate teacher. Even as He was dying, Jesus gave us lessons of incalculable worth, proving that, even in death, He could teach practical principles for meaningful existence. *Lessons From A*

Dying Savior seeks to capture the quintessential teachings that Jesus gave while on the cross.

There are several inexhaustible lessons that our Lord and Savior taught us during His suffering. These lessons were given in at least seven statements while Jesus was on the cross. The chapters in this book are arranged to follow the traditionally accepted order of Jesus' last words from the cross. Each chapter will highlight a lesson from our Lord. At the end of each chapter, the reader will find questions to facilitate reflection on and application of our Lord's lessons.

Chapter One considers the Savior's lesson on forgiveness. Chapter Two considers the Savior's lesson on compassion. Chapter Three considers the Savior's lesson on the family. Chapter Four considers the Savior's lesson on feeling forsaken. Chapter Five considers the Savior's lesson on being thirsty. Chapter Six considers the Savior's lesson on being triumphant. Chapter Seven considers the Savior's lesson on being in God's hands. Finally, Chapter Eight considers the Savior's consummate lesson on hope.

When properly applied, these lessons from our Savior and the way He died will teach us how to live. Through these lasting lessons, our Savior will teach us to be equipped to serve, suffer, surrender and succeed. May all who read this work be equipped, enriched and enlarged by these *Lessons From A Dying Savior.*

Chapter One: A Lesson on Forgiveness

Imagine. Imagine being born into poverty. Imagine having a dirty stable as your first nursery and a cow trough as your first cradle and crib. As a growing child, think about being misunderstood by your parents. Now, capture the idea of going away for eighteen years to prepare yourself to return and help your community. Think about what it would be like when you returned and were rejected by your own people.

Consider the joy of indelibly affecting people's lives. Then, juxtapose that joy with the sorrow of being judged and condemned for your words and actions even though your purpose is to help others. Contemplate hand-picking twelve men with whom you would live and serve for three and a half years, only to have one deny you, another betray you, and the rest forsake you when you needed them most. What would it have been like to be sentenced to death – even though you were innocent – while a guilty person was set free?

Finally, imagine being beaten with a whip that has bone and metal at the end of it. That whip literally tears your flesh every time it hits your skin. Imagine being nailed to a wooden cross with spikes in your hands and feet. Think about being spat upon, pierced in the side, mocked, and crowned with thorns. What would you say as you beheld your accusers, your antagonists, and your assassins while you died?

Would you be able and willing to forgive them and seek God's forgiveness on their behalf? Well, let us bring it a bit closer to home. How have you handled being hurt by others– whether physically, mentally, emotionally, financially or even spiritually? Were you willing to forgive the party that hurt you? Even more, could you intercede on their behalves for God's forgiveness? Chances are, most of us have great difficulty extending forgiveness to those who hurt, disappoint, betray, deny, abandon, and/or reject us. Therefore, we need help.

However, we do not need just any kind of help. We do not need theoretical or experiential help. We need assistance from someone who has dealt with the cruelty of his enemies. We need the aid of one of who has proven that it is possible to forgive your enemies, even while they hurt you.

In our first lesson in this book, we will look to the cross and learn a lesson on forgiveness.

A Lesson on Forgiveness

First, it is very important that we notice to whom Jesus directed His attention. He said, "Father…." He did not address His accusers or dignify His enemies with attention or direct discourse. Jesus set His gaze and conversation heavenward. Jesus prayed for God to forgive them. He held death at bay and overlooked His physical pain long enough to pray for His enemies. What a lesson on forgiveness this is!

Jesus teaches at least four things about forgiveness.

First, if we are going to really learn about true forgiveness, we must understand that *forgiveness is unselfish*.

Though He was an innocent man being persecuted, Jesus never expressed self-pity or highlighted His own painful predicament. Although He could have, He did not even try to invoke the pity of God on His behalf. Rather than focusing on Himself or His pain, Jesus turned His gaze towards heaven and said, "Father, forgive them...." When He spoke to God, it was not for Himself, but for *them*. If you and I are to practice true forgiveness, no matter how painful it maybe, we must understand that we cannot forgive and be selfish at the same time.

Yes, people have hurt us.
Yes, people have betrayed us.
Yes, people have disappointed us.
Yes, people have denied us.
Yes, people have rejected us.

However, this is not about us! It is about their need for God's forgiveness.

Jesus says that if you are going to forgive, then you need to pay attention to the way that He dealt with His pain, and the way that He dealt with those who inflicted unspeakable cruelty on Him.

Inevitably, human beings will try to see themselves as exceptions to the rule. "You don't know what happened. My father never owned me. He rejected me." There are no exceptions. There is only one answer. Jesus made that clear. We need to pray that God will forgive whoever has hurt us.

"But you don't understand. That man raped me!" Again, the more appalling the behavior, the more desperately the person needs God's forgiveness.

Someone else may say, "You don't know all of the hurt that I've experienced. You don't know the emotional trauma that I've been through. You don't know the sociological trauma that I've experienced. I should be in a crazy house right now, in the psychiatric ward." The only thing that will set you free from your misery is to pray for God's forgiveness.

What we must understand is that healing from our pain cannot fully take place until we are willing to look at our victimizers and say, "In Jesus' name, I want you to be forgiven by God. Yes, I hurt. Yes, I'm in pain. Yes, I despise what you did to me. But because you did it to me, that says something is wrong with you. And you need God's forgiveness." *It is unselfish,* which leads me to the second point.

Not only does Jesus teach us that forgiveness is unselfish, He also teaches us that *we must not seek vengeance.* The root word here is *avenge,* which comes from the Latin words *ad + vengier,* which together mean, "to vindicate." When you are truly

willing and ready to forgive, you will
understand that the act of forgiveness is
not about seeking revenge or vindication.
You do not desire that whatever they have
done to you will, in turn, happen to them.
You do not want them to hurt because they
hurt you. You do not wish bankruptcy on
them because they stole from you. Since
forgiveness is not about vengeance, you
should not seek vengeance.

Jesus said simply, "Father, forgive them,
for they know not what they are doing"
(Luke 23:34). He could have said, "Father
you've got legions of angels, and right now
I want you to send them down and wipe
out my assassins. I want you to unleash the
heavenly host and I want you to kill the
people who are trying to kill me." He had
the authority, the right, and He could have
easily said it –but He chose not to say it.
Jesus knew that we needed to learn that real
forgiveness is neither selfish nor vengeful.

Thirdly, when Jesus said, "Father, forgive
them; for they know not what they are
doing," He was telling us that forgiveness is
about understanding.

It is unselfish, it is not vengeful, and it is understanding.

You may be asking yourself why or how forgiveness shows understanding. To answer those questions, it is important to know that Jesus understood what they did not understand; otherwise He would not have been prompted to make such an unselfish, merciful plea.

Jesus understood that something was awry within mankind. He understood the wickedness that was within them and that they had been overtaken by evil. Yet, while we may feel disgust towards the Roman soldiers who crucified our Lord, they really represent you and me. Before Christ saved us, we crucified Him daily. We denied Him daily. We rejected Him every single day. We abandoned Him. We disappointed Him. Nevertheless, He understood that something was wrong with us on the inside. The only way that we could be delivered was for Him to say, "Father forgive them for they know not what they are doing."

Jesus had to suffer the penalty of death, (and God permitted Him to go through it) because His pain would be redemptive for the entire world. Even the very men who

were crucifying Him could be redeemed by
His actions.

Forgiveness is about understanding.

Do you think that the Jewish members
of the Sanhedrin Council, who conspired to
have Jesus convicted, would have
sanctioned His crucifixion if they really
understood who He was? Remember, the
Jews were waiting and looking for the
Messiah. They were looking for the
Messiah of Yahweh, the Messiah of God's
people. They were looking for a strong,
powerful, military, politically powerful man
who would come and rid them of all of
their enemies. They wanted a warrior who
would come and rule with an iron fist and a
mighty sword. They did not realize that the
very one for whom they had waited was the
man whom they demanded be crucified.
They did not understand that the very
Messiah they anticipated would be subject
to a harsh and brutal death at their hands.
Barabbus, a guilty man, would go free.
    If we are going to learn the lesson on
forgiveness, not only must we understand
that it is *unselfish*, that is not *vengeful*, and that

is *understanding*, but we should celebrate that true forgiveness is *undiluted*.

Forgiveness is undiluted.

To dilute something is to weaken it or water it down. When Jesus said, "Father, forgive *them*...," He was not just talking about the soldiers and accusers who put Him on the cross and mocked Him as He died. He looked beyond them. He looked down the corridors of time to see *us*. Two thousand years down the road, His forgiveness for our sins is just as powerful and real for us as it was at that moment on Calvary. Jesus saw the Roman soldiers, but He also saw us as He hung His head and said, "Father, forgive them, for they know not what they do." I know that there are great challenges when we try to forgive. Things like betrayal, abuse and abandonment are so personally overwhelming that we are challenged to remember what Jesus called us to do. But no matter how serious and how sinister the ordeal is, Jesus says, "Father, forgive them, for they know not what they do." If you do not know Christ, then you will never know forgiveness in this way, nor be able to extend it in this way.

The lesson is easy to understand, but it is hard to apply. Nevertheless, the same Christ who prayed for His enemies while He was dying lives in us.

He knew that He had to die because sinners were unable to save themselves. He knew that without the shedding of blood, there could be no forgiveness of sin. But, He also knew that His request of the Father would be granted for the following reasons:

The blood had been shed.

The lamb without spot or blemish had been provided.

The atonement for sin had been made.

The debt of sin had been paid.

The law had been fulfilled.

The master plan had been completed.

The future of souls in need of forgiveness had been   made clear.

All of this came as the result of a prayer from a dying Savior.

Jesus prayed for me. He prayed for you. He had you on His mind. Despite His pain, agony, and dying status, He prayed,

"Father, forgive them, for they know not what they are doing."

This is the first lesson from a dying Savior — *A Lesson on Forgiveness.*

If we are true Christians, then we have to learn and practice this lesson on forgiveness. This is a hard lesson. We cannot pick and choose whom we are willing to forgive. We must forgive whoever is in need of it, whether it is a relative, a friend, a colleague or a stranger.

Forgiveness should be *unselfish*, not *vengeful, understanding* and *undiluted.*

Because the same Christ who prayed for His enemies (while He was yet dying) lives in us, we can count on His help and extend our forgiveness to others. We all need forgiveness! We who have been the recipient of Christ's forgiveness have a duty to extend that blessing. We need to include even those who hurt, disappoint, deny, betray, or reject us. That is why He prayed, "Father forgive them, for they know not what they are doing." Jesus knew something that even his antagonists and assassins did not know— that sinners could never get to heaven by good works. He knew that sinners were doomed to eternal damnation without a onetime, eternal sacrifice. He knew that sinners' inability to save themselves was the reason that He had to die. He knew without the shedding of blood, that there could be no forgiveness for sins.

He also knew that His request of the Father would be granted because His blood had been shed. The lamb without spot or blemish had been provided. The atonement for sin had been made. The debt for sin had been paid. The law had been fulfilled. The master plan had been completed. The requirements had been met. The future of souls in need of forgiveness had been made clear.

All this came as a result of a prayer from a dying Savior.

Lessons on Forgiveness

1. How do you define forgiveness?

2. Does your definition match what Jesus modeled on the cross?

3. Where is forgiveness discussed in the New Testament? (Matt. 18:21-35; Col. 3:13)

4. What has been your greatest challenge regarding forgiveness?

5. Have you ever asked God to forgive you? If so, what difference did it make in your life? If you have not, remember that you can do so right now! God loves you and promises to forgive all those who ask. (1 John 1:9)

6. If you had been in Jesus' place, could you have freely extended forgiveness the way He did?

7. How can you be more forgiving of others and yourself? (Ultimately, the failure to forgive will rob *you* of health, joy, peace and progress. Read and remember God's word through the Apostle Paul in Phil. 4:13.)

Chapter Two: A Lesson On Compassion

Why do we pay little or no attention to the victims of AIDS? Unfortunately, it is not until someone close to us is diagnosed as HIV positive that we show compassion. Why are we unconcerned about finding a cure for cancer until a close friend or family member begins to suffer with it? Why are we devoid of compassion for the homeless until homelessness affects us personally? Why do we forget our compassion and stand in condemnation toward people who suffer from substance abuse?

My brothers and my sisters, there *is* a malady that is adversely affecting people in this society that should pull at the heartstrings of Christians. Our society has lost its sense of compassion toward all human beings. There was a time when it was unnecessary to personally know the person whose son was hit by a car in order to offer our assistance. There was a time when we did not need to know someone personally in order to pray for him or her. There was a time when compassion was inextricably bound to the heartstrings of believers in Christ Jesus.

Today, even Christians are often devoid of compassion unless the crisis directly affects them or someone close to them. This attitude is inconsistent with the teaching of Jesus Christ.

I believe that the Lord wanted this book written so that we can restore compassion as a constant in our lives, our communities, and in our churches. It should not matter who the victim is, or whether we know them personally. Our mere knowledge of another's plight should be enough for us to show compassion. Our compassion should inspire us to help anyone with a legitimate need, even a stranger.

Jesus is our example of this act. Even as Jesus was dying, He helped a stranger.

Our dying Savior wanted us to receive His lesson on compassion.

The Bible reveals that Jesus exemplified and personified compassion to others. There were at least four things that Jesus did for a stranger as acts of compassion while dying on the cross. As we observe His situation, it is important to remember that Jesus was in no physical position to help the man who hung beside him; they were *both* dying on the cross. Consider that one dying man is looking upon another dying man, and Jesus has the heart to show compassion!

There is a lesson in this fact: you do not need to be "up" in order to help someone who is down. Life brings many burdens, as well as blessings. You can come along someone's side and deliver compassion – even if you are facing your own challenges. One of the blessings of giving compassion is that it makes you feel better too!

Many of us make the mistake of believing that we have to have certain resources or positions of influence or status to alleviate another person's suffering. But God expects that we who have received His compassion will share that compassion with others.

Jesus exemplifies and personifies compassion in the text. Through His example, we will learn how we can and should do the same.

Observe the first thing that Jesus does on the cross to show compassion: He acknowledges the man's request.

The man on the cross next to Jesus is a criminal. Another man on a third cross mocks Jesus, saying, "Aren't you the Christ? Save yourself and us!" (Luke 23:39b). But the man to whom we commonly refer as the thief on the cross looked at the other one and told him to be quiet! He knew that they deserved their punishment. They had broken the law. Even more, he also knew that Jesus had done nothing wrong.

Somehow, this stranger saw God in the man that hung between him and the other criminal, at which point he respectfully turned and said, "Jesus, remember me when you come into your kingdom" (Luke 23:42). In essence, he was saying, "I am not asking that you take me with you. All I want is just to be remembered. My family has forgotten about me. My friends have forsaken me. Everybody has left me to die on the cross by myself. I just want you to remember me. Just remember me."

The fact that Jesus spoke to him was an acknowledgment of the man's request. Contemplate this for a moment: There was a sign that hung over Jesus' head on the cross. In Hebrew, Latin and Greek, it proclaimed, "**KING OF THE JEWS.**"

That was an inexpressible understatement, for Jesus was King of the Jews, *and* King of Kings. So remember, Jesus was under no obligation to respond to this man. Even so, He responded to the thief, but not by saying, "I'm busy with my own pain. How dare you ask Me to remember you? My own friends have forsaken Me. I poured my life into them for three and half years. I tried to do all I could and no one, save John, came to the cross. Be quiet!"

Jesus could have said, "I don't have time to respond to your request. I'm trying to die. I'm trying to get this done and over with. I've got to suffer; I know I've got to suffer, so just let Me get it done and over with." He also could have exclaimed, "Do you know whom you are talking to? Do you know who I am? I am no mere peasant! I am the Prince of Peace." Instead, Jesus turned and spoke to the man, saying, "I tell you the truth, today you will be with me in paradise" (Luke 23:43). In doing so, Jesus acknowledged his request.

Here is a question for you to ponder. When was the last time someone was in pain and made a request of you? What was your response? Did you condemn them, or did you respond with compassion?

If you and your spouse exchanged hurtful words the last time you argued, what was your response when your partner apologized? When you were asked to forgive and forget, did you say, "No, I'm not going to forget about it? You hurt me. How am I going to forgive you when I'm hurting? How can I extend anything to you when I'm hurting?" Or, did you say, "We've both been hurt. Let's forgive each other and move on?"

I am talking about showing real, everyday compassion! And yes, it can be really hard to do because your heart wants to hold onto all the wrongs in your life. Let them go! Compassion is what we are called to do. Let's go about the business of extending it.

Ponder this: When was the last time you met a homeless person who asked you for something to eat as you were leaving a restaurant? Did you tell them that you were on your way to work? Did you tell them that it was *your* lunch hour? Did you tell them you had no change? Remember, they did not ask you for change; they asked you for some food. Did you just walk away, or did you turn to them and take whatever you had to buy them food? If you acknowledged their plight – even if you just offered a burger or biscuit – then it was an act of compassion. That is what Jesus did. He acknowledged the thief's request.

But Jesus did more than just acknowledge the man's request; He acted upon the man's request.

It is one thing to acknowledge a request; it is another thing to act upon it. Compassion is about action.

Compassion will cause you to move beyond just vague concern. Compassion catapults you into action. Real compassion is where words and ways are wed. It is proof that your self-advertisements are real. Hence, when Jesus says to him, "Verily, I say to thee today that thou shalt be with me in paradise," we see how His concern has catapulted Him to contribution.

He acted upon the man's request.

It is not enough to say, "I'll pray for you," if someone needs compassionate action! If somebody needs food, and you have food, do not tell him or her, "I'll pray for you." *Feed them*! If they need help paying an electricity bill and you can spare the money, give it to them. Or, if necessary, go and pay the bill for them. Do not leave them in the dark. Show compassion by acting on the person's request.

God has given you many blessings. Prove your compassion by giving.

Talk is cheap. We run around talking about what we could do, what we ought to do, and what the "Christian thing" is to do. Yet, seldom do we actually do anything! Jesus showed us how to seize the opportunity to make an eternal difference in someone's life. We must learn from Jesus.

When this century began, people ran around in a panic. Some people panicked over food. Some panicked over money. Some panicked over clothing. Some panicked over transportation. Others panicked over the potential need for safe housing. How shameful it would have been if the world finally came to the house of God and, when the people of God were asked for assistance, the response was, "We'll pray for you." The church should be equipped and willing to help people, not just acknowledge them.

Jesus *acts* after He acknowledges the man's request. But His compassion did not stop there! True compassion exceeds the boundaries of what the need is and deals with who is in need." Therefore, Jesus does a third thing from the cross to show compassion:

He accepted the man making the request.

We cannot separate the need from the person who is in need. For instance, you cannot be concerned about homelessness without also being concerned about the holistic well being of the individuals who are homeless. The two are inextricably bound to one another. Jesus did not simply say, "Okay, I'll remember you, but don't even think about going to heaven with me." He did not say, "Okay, I'll remember you when I get into my Kingdom. In the meantime, I'm leaving you here to be miserable. Deal with it." He did not say, "Even though I'm going to meet your need later on, I don't want anything to do with you right now."

Jesus said, "…today you will be with me in Paradise

In essence, He said, "I accept you."

Yes, you may be a criminal.

Yes, you may be incarcerated because you broke the law.

Yes, you may have done wrong in your life.

Yes, you had a lot of filth in your life.

Yes, you may have a lot of skeletons in your closet.

But right now, because you turned to me for help, I accept you. Because I accept you, you can be with me." Jesus says, "Just being in my presence will relieve all of your needs."

Dear friend, Jesus says to you and me that our past is inconsequential when we turn to Him. In the blink of an eye, Jesus can change your life. If, like the thief on the cross, you turn to Him, Jesus will replace your guilt with forgiveness, your dark past with a bright future, your delinquency with credit, your sorrow with joy, your confusion with order, and your doom with deliverance. Jesus can and will do more than you can imagine or expect. Remember, He is not preoccupied with your needs. Jesus is preoccupied with *you*. He wants to show you compassion so that you can do the same for others. Jesus showed true compassion after He accepted the man who made the request. Jesus acknowledged the man's needs, and acted upon his request. But consider the fourth and final exciting thing that He did on the cross to show compassion:

He assured the man of more than he requested.

In Luke 23:42, all the man asked was to be remembered when Jesus got into the kingdom. He did not ask to get into the kingdom; he just petitioned to be remembered. Jesus did more than the man requested. Your Bible says, "Jesus answered him, I tell you the truth, today you will be with me in paradise." Essentially, Jesus was saying, "Not only will I remember you, but to make sure I never forget you, I'm going to keep you with me." Jesus assured the man of more than he requested. And if Jesus can do that for a stranger, then what can His own expect?

The New Testament book of Colossians says we were enemies of God. We were aliens and strangers to God. Therefore, the thief on the cross really represents *us*. If Jesus can do it for us, then what should we do for somebody else? If Jesus asks us to go one mile, then we should go two miles. If someone asks for a shirt, then we should give him or her a coat as well. He assured the man of more than He requested. He said you only asked to be remembered, but I am going to let you remain with Me. Since you are dying with Me, I am going to permit you to live again with Me.

Jesus' lesson on compassion is a simple one for Christians. The crux of the lesson is this: Christ showed compassion for us by giving His life on the cross. Likewise, we, as the recipients of His compassion, should share the same compassion with others. After all, that is why He died on the cross. He did it out of compassion for us — in spite of our unworthiness.

He acknowledged our need. We needed the ultimate sacrifice. We needed a sacrifice of a lamb without a spot or blemish. For those reasons, He died for us. He knew we could not save ourselves, so He chose to lay down His life for us. In the book of John, Jesus said, "The reason my Father loves me is that I lay down my life — only to take it up again. No one takes it from me, but I lay it down of my own accord" (John 10:17,18).

He acknowledges our needs. He acts on our needs. He accepts us along with our needs. He looked down the turnpike of time and saw that there would be a Claybon Lea, Jr. who would need some compassion. He also looked down the turnpike of time and saw you.

After He accepts us, He assures us that we will not only be remembered, but that we will also have everlasting life in heaven. In that same tenth chapter in the Gospel of John, Jesus promises that He would also give us life more abundantly while on earth and life everlasting in heaven. Now that is good news!

Jesus' unselfish, sacrificial act of compassion reminds me of a story I once heard.

A little boy was out playing in the local park. He was always fond of dogs, but his father never allowed him to have one. That day, there was a tan-colored dog in the park. It was filthy with mange and so badly bruised that it could only walk on three legs. But the little boy saw something that pulled at his heartstrings. He looked for a name-tag to identify the dog's owner, but found none. So he took the dog back home.

The little boy was sitting on the stoop playing with the dog when his father came out and said, "Son, what are you doing?"

Clinging to the dog, the boy replied cautiously, "Well, Daddy, I found this dog."

His father was not happy. He instructed, "Well son, you need to let that dog go."

The boy held tighter. He respected his Daddy, but he knew there was something special about the dog.

The father said, "No, son. Look at the dog. It is dirty, filthy, and mangy. Its hair is matted, it stinks, and it seems to have a bruised leg. Maybe I'll get you a dog sometime, but you've got to let that dog go. You don't know what kind of diseases that dog has. It may have rabies. You don't know where it has been, and you don't know what it has been doing."

But the little boy was persistent. He said, "No Daddy, I've got to have this dog. I know he looks mangy, I know he looks dirty, I know he looks filthy, I know he smells and I know he has a bruised leg, but Daddy I've got to have this dog."

His father thought for a moment then asked, "Well, son, what you see in this dog?"

"Well, Daddy," he answered, "I know he is dirty right now, but if I wash him, I believe he will be clean. He'll look better and he'll smell better. And, Daddy, if I take a little piece of wood and take some tape and wrap it around his leg, I believe that he will be able to walk using his own strength in a few weeks."

The father looked at him and said, "Son, I think you still need to get rid of the dog."

The boy urged, "No, I see something in this dog and I've got to have this dog."

Moved by the compassion that his son had for this lost, filthy, mangy, injured dog, he shook his head, but helped him bandage up the dog's leg.

Just as his son said, the dog's leg got better. After he was washed, a beautiful coat appeared. He was no longer filthy, mangy, or matted. In the end, the father received the dog as a part of the family because of the compassion his son showed.

We are saved today because the Father was moved by the compassion of the Son.

JESUS PAID IT ALL
ALL TO HIM I OWE
SIN HAD LEFT A CRIMSON STAIN
HE WASHED IT WHITE AS SNOW

Lessons On Compassion

1. How can simply speaking to or acknowledging someone's request be a display of compassion?

2. James 2:14-18 mirrors the action that Jesus takes with the thief on the cross. Both Jesus and James teach us that true compassion moves beyond mere acknowledgment. How can your contributions to others show Christ-like compassion?

3. When and how has the Lord shown compassion toward you? What did it teach you about true compassion, in spite of your sins and shortcomings?

4. Is it easy or difficult for you to extend compassion to others who are suffering due to their own activity or irresponsibility? Why?

5. What role does unselfishness play in one's ability to be truly compassionate? (Luke10:25-37)

6. Since you have received the compassion of the Lord, to whom do you need to offer the same compassion you have been given? Now that Jesus has done it for you, follow His example. Be the compassion of the Lord in someone else's life today.

Chapter Three: A Lesson For The Family

We are going to look at another lesson Jesus gave us from the cross. It is a lesson about the family. In John 19:23-27, Jesus was hanging on the cross and was in the process of dying. He looked at the inevitable end of His life from a human perspective. He took time while on the cross to pay attention to the needs of others. In His first utterance from the cross, He beheld His assassins, His mockers, and His revilers and spoke to the Father on their behalf. He prayed, "Father, forgive them, for they know not what they are doing" (Luke 23:34). He then turned His attention to the needs of a thief on the cross, who petitioned Him, "When you come into your kingdom, remember me." Jesus did not rebuke him. Jesus did not bring the man's attention to His suffering. Instead, Jesus responded to the man with words that exceeded his expectations. He looked upon him with compassion and said, "...today you will be with me in paradise" (Luke 23:43). While Jesus is yet dying, He teaches us about the significance of others!

As one of my colleagues, Kevin Jones, has said, "Jesus had some unfinished business." As He perused the crowd that surrounded the cross, Jesus saw His mother and John at the foot of the cross. At that point, Jesus discovered that there was some unfinished business pertaining to His own family. He focuses on the two people who were probably the most precious to Him during His earthly pilgrimage. First, there was His mother Mary, the woman whom God blessed and chose to bring His body into the world. This was the same Mary, who took Him to Simeon so that He might be dedicated to God; and the woman who hurried back to the temple to find her child, then heard Him say, "Didn't you know I had to be in my Father's house" (Luke 2:49)? It was His mother who accompanied Jesus to His first miracle at the wedding feast in Canaan of Galilee, where He turned water into wine. Mary gave birth to Him, and John says Mary stood at the foot of the cross and remained there while her son died. Can you imagine what she had to be going through?

Next, Jesus looked down at John, the one whom the Bible says Jesus loved. It was not that He did not love the other disciples, but there was a special place in Jesus' heart for John. After all, you must remember, that John was one of Jesus' first disciples. Along with Peter, Andrew and James, John was one of the first four whom Jesus chose to be one of His disciples. John accompanied Jesus when He went up on the Mount of Transfiguration. John went with Jesus to the Garden of Gethsemane and was assigned to intercessory prayer. John remained loyal to Him. John did not betray Him and he did not deny Jesus. He loved John. It was John who sat next to Him at the Last Supper while Judas, the betrayer, sat on the other side. And it was John who was close enough to lay his head on Jesus' breast.

The Bible does not say so, but we can inferentially gather that John was probably Jesus' best earthly friend. So now, picture this scenario. We have a son and a Savior on the cross. We have a mother looking at her son who is in the throes of death. Then we have a friend who came in spite of the fact that all of the other disciples ran away when Jesus needed them most. At this moment, Jesus chooses to teach us the first of three things about the family: family devotion.

Particularly, note the devotion of Jesus' mother. Mary could have run away. Mary could have decided that she could not bare the pain of seeing her son crucified. She could have hidden like the others, but because of her devotion to Him, she was loyal and committed.

Today, families are enduring such negative events, situations and feelings that devotion has been discarded. Some parents forsake their children when their children need them the most. The family unit is not what Christ meant it to be.

On the cross, He showed us what the family unit should be like. Despite the darkness and the excruciating pain, *Jesus and Mary* remained loyal and faithful.

So, if your son or daughter is out of church, remain devoted. If they are addicted to drugs or struggling with alcohol, remain devoted to them. If they have chosen an alternative lifestyle, remain devoted to them. These are your children! You do not have to approve of what *they do* in order to be faithful and loyal *to whom and whose they are.* Mary models the devotion that we ought to have within our family.

The second thing we see here is duty to family. Whereas devotion means living with purposeful commitment, loyalty, and faithfulness, duty is commitment tied to responsibility. Many of us accept devotion but reject responsibility and duty. Yet, while dying on the cross, Jesus showed His mother love, by fulfilling His duty to her. He made sure someone would take care of her. He said to her, "Woman, I know that your heart is aching and wrenching. I know that there is a hole in your heart because your son is being vilified and crucified. I will make sure you are taken care of in life, just as I will take care of you in death."

I encourage you to be emotionally present for your family and dutiful as you fulfill your responsibilities. Do not throw your parents away! And do not abandon your grandparents when they get old. If Jesus could look out for His mother in His death, what should we do for our families while we are yet living?

My heart ached when I recently visited someone at the hospital. A lady walked into the lobby and immediately recognized two of the ladies who were with me. We asked how she was doing and why she was at the hospital. She told us that her father had Alzheimer's and had to be restrained at home. She was trying to take care of him. Then her mother was admitted into the hospital, and the doctors informed her that her mother would have to stay with another family member, or be admitted into a nursing home. While my heart was aching, I also felt tremendous admiration for this woman. She is in her fifties and has seven children of her own. Nevertheless, she has enough duty in her heart and mind to make sure that she has taken care of her ailing parents. Her story is similar to what Jesus did.

As He died on the cross, Jesus made plans about who would take care of His mother. Jesus said, "Woman, behold thy son," meaning that He was commending her to John. Mary was to hold John as her own son, and John was to take care of her as he would his own mother. John would also help her with Jesus' other siblings since His father, Joseph, was already dead. Jesus wanted to make sure that He took responsibility for His family.

Dear friends, it is critical that we exhibit family duty and take responsibility for those who are dear to us. There is no time to hold grudges or harp on issues from the past. We must put our personal differences aside and uphold high the principles of devotion and duty.

As noted, family devotion and duty are clearly demonstrated. The third thing that gives us hope is that Jesus shows us family deliverance. Jesus gives John to Mary as her son, and He's so concerned about the family unit remaining intact that He gives John, his friend, a mother. He delivers the family from dissolution. Through His actions, we are taught that no matter what our losses may be, God knows how to lift up somebody else so that they can step up and take the place of a family member who can no longer be there. That is the deliverance for the family that Jesus has guaranteed on the cross. Even in our loss, He guarantees some gain. Jesus said, "Woman behold thy son." Then, He looked at John and said, "Behold thy mother." From that time forward, the disciple took her into his home. It is implied that they lived together until Mary's death as a family, as mother and son. There was deliverance for His family.

God knows how to fill the void in our lives. It does not matter if you have lost a son or daughter, a mother or father, a sister or brother, or friend. God knows how to move somebody else to step into your life.

Some years ago, Dr. Martin Luther King, Jr. was invited to speak at Morehouse College, his alma mater. By then, he was in the midst of the Civil Rights struggle. There was a delay, and all of the participants were asked to wait in the cafeteria. When he entered, Dr. King heard a woman moaning in a corner. Dr. King walked over to her and asked, "Madam, is everything all right?"

"Oh, Dr. King," she said, "everything's all right. I'm not moaning because anything's wrong, I'm moaning because I've just been thinking about and reflecting on God's deliverance and how God knows how to make a way." She continued, "Dr. King, my husband died some years ago. Recently, I lost my one and only son, and it hurt me to my heart. Dr. King, I was so distraught. I was so depressed over what I viewed as the destruction of my family that when I went to bed a few nights ago, I prayed to God and asked him not to let me wake up on this side of the Jordan.

But Dr. King, I went to sleep, and the next morning I woke up, and I need to confess that I was a little upset with God, because I asked him to take me since He had broken up my family. I was all right when my husband went because at least I had my son, but now my son was gone and there was nobody left but me." She said, "But Dr. King, as I lay there on the pillow not wanting to get up out of the bed, I heard something through the pillow that kept on saying, 'Be not dismayed whatever betides.' Dr. King, I couldn't stay there. I wanted to stay there, but I couldn't stay in the bed, so I got up and I walked into the bathroom and washed my face and brushed my teeth. I turned the faucets on and I could not hear the water hitting the sink because something just kept ringing in my ears, 'Be not dismayed whatever betides.'

"Then Dr. King, I went into the kitchen. I turned on the stove and I placed some bacon in the skillet. But I could not hear the crackling of the bacon because something just kept on ringing in my ears. 'Be not dismayed, whatever betides.' Dr. King, I finally finished making my breakfast, and I sat down at the table and low and behold, the doorbell rang. I went to the door and there was a tall, young gentleman at the door. He said, 'Ma'am, I know you don't really know me. I grew up with your son. He was my very best friend, and the way he talked about you, I feel in my heart as if you are my mother. I made a promise to your son that, if anything were to ever happen to him, I would do my best to take care of his mother. I heard that he died, but I was overseas and I couldn't make it to the funeral. But I'm here now, *mom*. I'm here as your son, and I accept you as my mother.'

"The man pulled out a check and said, 'Here, *mom*, I know it is rough, but I just want to take care of you.' Dr. King, I looked at the check. It was for $25,000! I started rejoicing. Tears rolled down my cheeks. He gave me his business card. He said, 'Now *mom*, if you need me morning, noon or night, give me a call. I can be reached 24 hours a day, 7 days a week, and I'll come running. If your money gets low, you let me know. I'll take care of you. If you have a bill due, let me know and I'll take care of you.'

"The young man turned around and he walked away. He got in his automobile and he turned on the engine." But, Dr. King, you know what? As the young man drove away, I couldn't even hear the roar of his automobile because as I stood in the doorway, I just heard in my mind, "Be not dismayed whatever betides.' God will take care of you. Beneath his wings of love abides. God will take care of you every day along the way. He will take care of you. Don't be dismayed. Don't worry or fret. God will take care of you."

This is a wondrous illustration of what God can do for our family through devotion, duty and deliverance. Even when the family circle is broken, God will mend that circle and cause that void to be filled if we trust in Him and remember that He takes personal responsibility for the family unit. He, thereby, commits Himself to the deliverance and the sustaining of the family.

As Jesus hung on the cross, He said these things: The first was, "Father, forgive them, for they know not what they are doing" (Luke 23:34). Next, He said to a thief who was experiencing capital punishment by crucifixion next to Him, "…today you will be with me in paradise" (Luke 23:43). Then, Jesus beheld his best friend and beloved disciple, John, who was about to become friendless, and his mother, who was about to lose her son, and joined them together.

The first words of our Savior from the cross were directed toward other people's needs. When He said, "Father forgive them…" He was not asking forgiveness for Himself; He had committed no sin. When He looked at the man who hung beside Him and uttered, "…be with Me in Paradise," He saw a need for this man's salvation. When He looked at His mother and best friend, Jesus saw a need to make a potentially disjointed family become a delivered family. He sought to make certain that they would have an intact family.

Lessons For the Family

1. What three things does Jesus teach us about family in this chapter?

2. What have been your greatest challenges with your family? Have any of your struggles been in the three areas that Jesus teaches and models in this chapter?

3. Family was obviously important to Jesus. How much of a priority should the family be to us?

4. How has the Lord filled a void in your family?

5. Review the text selected as the foundation for this chapter. What family is the Lord placing you in to fill a void as he did with Mary and John?

6. What can you do to better value and bless the family that the Lord has given you? (Deut. 5:16; Eph. 5:25-30)

Chapter Four: A Lesson On Feeling Forsaken

Immediately after Jesus attended to the needs of others, it became dark. While He was ministering to others, the sun was shining. Now that He had addressed the needs of others, there was midnight at midday. Jesus turned His focus towards the real purpose of His crucifixion: He had to die to pay the penalty for sin, past, present and future, for all mankind. The darkness was not an eclipse. Instead, it was the manifestation of God's inability to look upon sin.

God could not look upon sin, even as it covered His own Son. God cannot tolerate sin. God removed the glory of His face from focusing on Jesus Christ. Consequently, darkness fell as He hung on the cross. Because Jesus had never experienced this before, He cried out, "My God, My God, why have you forsaken me?" (Matthew 27:46).

We have all felt that way at times. We feel like God is nowhere to be found. I would venture to say that, at some point in our lives, the majority of us have experienced the same type of feeling that Jesus experienced on the cross– forsaken.

The Greek word for forsaken means: "to be abandoned, to be left in dire straights, to be left in a helpless state, without resources." Think about what Jesus must have been experiencing! His cry confirms that He was Divine, but at the same time, flesh. He was holy, yet human.

In the Garden of Gethsemane, Jesus gave us an undeniable portrait of His humanity. When He was in the garden about to approach His suffering on the cross He said, "O my Father, if it is possible, let this cup pass from Me" (Matthew 26:39). On the cross, He showed the greatest portrait of His humanity when He cried out, (just as you or I would) "My God, My God, why have you forsaken me?"

It would have been enough if, John, who came at the last minute, had forsaken Him. It was enough that the same people that He had healed had forsaken Him. Of all those whom Jesus had freed from demonic possession, fed when hungry and resurrected when dead, none were there for Him in the end. All of that must have been irreconcilably hurtful. But when God appeared to forsake Jesus, how could He cope with such trauma?

You can deal with friends walking away. You can deal with your mother, father, sister or brother having a problem with you and walking away. You could also handle your resources disappearing. But one thing I do not think that any of us can deal with is experiencing the feeling of forsakenness—that terrible feeling when we believe that God is no longer present for us.

Though Jesus was lonely, He was not alone. He experienced physical anguish. What hurt Him and pierced His heart the most was the sense of spiritual detachment from the Father. But God had to forsake Him because of His own holiness. As explained in Second Corinthians 5:21, "God made Him who had no sin to be sin for us." Jesus, who knew no sin, became sin for us. Galatians 3:13 tells us, "Cursed is everyone who is hung on a tree." He became a curse for the cursed. We are the ones who should have been there, but He became our curse and the payment for our salvation. Jesus hung in our stead.

Because of His holiness, God could not look at us in our sin. When our sin was placed upon Christ, God could not look at

His Son either. He could not look at Jesus because of our humanity, and there had to be the shedding of blood for the remission of sins. We could not be saved if Jesus had not died, and if God had not dealt with sin justly.

While the relationship between the Father and Son was not broken, God had to turn away from Christ, even if only temporarily. He was still the Son. God was still the Father. But sin broke the fellowship and communion with God. So, when our sins were placed upon the Son, God could no longer look with affection toward the cross. If ever you feel forsaken by God, you might need to go back and examine your life. You might need to examine whether or not there are some things in your life that you have not confessed unto the Lord and repented. Notice I said confess *and* repent. Some of us apologize, but do not change our ways. If you repent, not only do you confess your wrongs and apologize, but you also turn away from them.

Whenever you find yourself in a spiritual wilderness, you might need to check your personal life and determine whether or not there is any sin that has fractured your fellowship with God. The devil himself is not capable of fracturing our relationship with God. The devil cannot separate us. The Apostle Paul said it best: "Neither height nor depth, nor anything else in all creation, will be able to separate us from the love of God that is in Christ Jesus our Lord" (Romans 8:39). The only thing that puts a barrier between God and us is our personal choice to live in sin.

You may ask, "If that's the case when I feel forsaken, then what should I do?" The first thing to do when you feel forsaken by God is to fortify your faith. Fortify, strengthen, bolster, and support your faith. Jesus never lost faith in God. He says, "My God, My God…" While He does not refer to God as Father because of the fracture in their fellowship, He yet owns God, as we all must. He uses the personal possessive pronoun, "my." He says, "…*My* God, why has thou forsaken Me?" He owns God as His own, which says that He does not lose faith in God.

More importantly, God never leaves Jesus. He just turns His face from Jesus. How could God leave His only son? Moreover, how could God go anywhere when He is everywhere at the same time? God does not forsake us in the sense of leaving us, but when our sin fractures our fellowship with Him; He must turn His face from us. It is up to us to reassess our own lives and fortify our faith in Him. We must minister to ourselves, and we must continue to put our trust in God. We also must remember that our suffering is not an eternal sentence.

Faith in action will cause you to look at what God has done and remember what He can do. When Jesus was in the Garden of Gethsemane, God did not relieve Him of the responsibility of going to the cross. Yet, God provided Him with what He needed to endure that period in time. God will do the same thing for you. Isaiah 40:31 says, "But they that wait upon the LORD shall renew their strength; they shall mount up with wings as eagles; they shall run, and not be weary; and they shall walk, and not faint." (KJV) Fortify your faith.

After you fortify your faith, then you must find a text, that is to say, use the scripture. We learn how to handle life's trials by discovering how Jesus handled His. As Jesus hung on the cross and the darkness prevailed, He fortified His faith. Read Psalm 22. In verse one, you will discover that in order to express what He was going through, Jesus reached back into the Old Testament text and pulled out words penned by David, the author of the Psalm, who also cried out, "My God, my God, why have you forsaken me?"

Finding and connecting with a text, the scripture will help you. In Romans 10:17, Paul says, "Consequently, faith comes from hearing the message, and the message is heard through the word of Christ." Jesus did not resort to feelings of self-pity because of the fractured fellowship with God. Jesus did not become depressed. He did not curse God. Instead, He found a text to fortify His faith and help Him make it through His darkest hour. I admonish you to do the same.

Whenever you feel that God has forsaken you, do not stop praying. Pray *harder*, even if you can only say, "My God, my God, why have you forsaken me?" When you are going through tough times, do not put down His Word! Find a text to guide you through the darkness. When you open your Bible, you might stumble upon a text that will remind you that, "Weeping may remain for a night, but rejoicing comes in the morning" (Psalm 30:5).

Your Bible is full of God's promises. If you look, you will find that there is plenty to keep you focused on Him. The Lord will also meet you right where you are. Tell the Lord, "I believe, but help my unbelief." In essence, when we are forsaken, we must fortify our faith. We must keep on trusting, believing and knowing that every situation in this life is temporary.

If you can hold on a little while longer, deliverance is coming. God will allow the clouds of darkness to disappear and the *S-O-N* will shine even if the sun does not. God will let the *Son* shine in your darkness. You will say, "Thank you, Lord, that you never left me, even when I thought you did. You never really forsook me. You just had to turn your face until my sin was dealt with."

Lessons On Feeling Forsaken

1. Have you ever been forsaken by family and friends? If so, describe how it made you feel.

2. Have you ever felt forsaken by God? If so, describe the experience.

3. What was the difference between being forsaken by others and feeling forsaken by God?

4. What did you learn about God when you looked back on a time when it seemed like God had forsaken you?

5. What did you learn from Jesus' experience of feeling forsaken by God at a critical hour?

6. What counsel would you give to someone who feels that God has forsaken him or her?

Chapter Five: A Lesson On Being Thirsty

Jesus had been on the cross for some six hours. The blood vessels in His body were almost dried up. Fever raged though Him. His was tongue now parched and cleaved to His jaw. The spiritual desolation expressed as He cried, "My God, my God, why has thou forsaken me?" had completely exhausted Him.

Eastern desert travelers can tell us what happens to people when they have no water. Their mouths bleed, their eyes bulge, and they utter hoarse, agony-filled cries as they try to fend off impending death.

By this time, Jesus was close to death. In the midst of His agony, He showed us the fullness of His humanness. Just as we would, He cried, "I thirst." He had already said, "Father, forgive them for they know not what they do." He had already said to the thief, "This day shall thou be with me in paradise." He had already said, "Woman, behold thy son! Son, behold thy mother!" He had already cried out unto God with a loud voice, "My God! My God! Why has thou forsaken me?"

After issuing this great cry, He whispered, "I thirst."

There are at least three major meanings behind His declaration. When we remember who it is that said these words, it becomes clear that His thirst symbolizes His complete acceptance of His sacrifice for us.

In the fourth chapter of John, Jesus told the woman at the well that, "I could give you water to drink and you'll never have to thirst again. I've got a river of life that springs up, in the everlasting life." He also said, "... everyone who thirsts, come and drink from a fountain that never runs dry." Jesus is the river of life and the source of all water. In the beginning, He spoke and caused His Spirit to move upon the firmament of the waters so that the world would exist. This same Jesus now said, "I thirst."

He is the source of all life. And yet, He cried, "I thirst." Although His life was coming to an earthly end, Jesus denied Himself by not using His omnipotence to save Himself. While He could have quenched His thirst, He chose to endure the agony so that we would have our

ultimate thirst quenched. He had to
experience excruciating suffering *for us.*

According to the scripture, He also
fulfilled prophesy through experiencing this
thirst.

In Psalm 69:3, 21, it was prophesied that
the Messiah would declare how parched
His mouth was, and that He would be
given gall and vinegar. Indeed, as indicated
in John 19:29, when He says, "I am
thirsty," the cruel soldiers around the cross
offered Him vinegar, which made it worse.

Jesus' destiny had been predicted
thousands of years prior to his actual
crucifixion. So as He allows the scriptures
to be fulfilled, we are delivered from
suffering in sin.

On the cross, Jesus did everything that
was foretold in the scriptures. He did
everything that was required of Him to
secure our salvation. The deliverance from
suffering is for Him. The deliverance from
sin was for *us.* He did not say, "I thirst,"
until all had been completed and the
scripture would be fulfilled.

When He said, "I thirst," He was really
summoning death to come and deliver Him
from His suffering. His suffering was on
two levels– spiritual and physical. It was

spiritual because God had to turn away from the sin Jesus had taken on for us. He experienced spiritual suffering because, for a time, He lost the fellowship with the Father. When you suffer from having your fellowship with God broken for any period of time, you will desire, like Jesus did, to be delivered from that suffering. He thirsted for God!

Jesus' spiritual thirst to save the souls of men and women also motivated Him. After anguishing over the thousands of years of animal sacrifices, He said, "I'm so thirsty for their salvation that I'll be the sacrifice. His anguish over animal sacrifices was due to their insufficiency to pay for all sin, once and for all (Heb. 10:1-7, 11-12). I will be parched, I will suffer, and I will experience anguish, just so that they might have a right to the tree of life."

He also desired deliverance from physical suffering. His earthly body could handle no more. He desired deliverance from suffering for Himself and also for humanity so that we might all be saved.

Yet, Jesus died in record time. The average person in Roman society who was crucified could actually live on the cross for two-three days before dying. But Jesus died in a matter of hours because death did not control Him. He controlled death to get to the point where He could say, "I thirst." His statement was death's cue to escort Jesus to the next point in His movement toward salvation.

What we discover in our investigation of His words, "I thirst," is that Jesus revealed His heart to us. He was passionate about wanting us all to be forever delivered from our sins. Jesus' words and actions also revealed after what things we should thirst. The problem in our society, even amongst believers in the Lord Jesus Christ, is that we very often try to fulfill and quench our thirst with things that cannot ultimately satisfy us.

We need to be thirsty for the right things, we need to go to the right place, and we need to do the right thing in order to truly quench our thirst. During His Sermon on the Mountain, (Matthew 5:6), Jesus tells us, "Blessed are those who hunger and thirst after righteousness." You ought to be thirsty for righteousness. Things of this world will not quench your thirst. No pay increase, promotion, material possession, or earthly being will quench your thirst. However, make certain that you thirst after righteousness. While there is nothing wrong with money, success or other people, those things cannot occupy the space where righteousness should live. If you thirst after righteousness, and allow that to be your passion, then you will *discover* what God teaches us in Mathew 5:16: "If you seek first the Kingdom of God and his righteousness, then all of these things shall be added unto you." Even in the Old Testament, God said in Psalm 37:4 that "If you delight yourself in the Lord, he'll give you the desires of your heart."

If you are thirsty this morning, then you need to thirst after righteousness. If you are thirsty this evening, do not go to the world to try to satisfy your thirst.

Jesus is the solution to our thirst.

Jesus declared Himself the solution to our thirst; He is water from which you can drink and never get thirsty again. He has a well of water that will never go dry. He beckons men and women to come unto Him saying, "All ye who are thirsting, I will give you drink."

If you need to know how, one of the hymn writers has told us. "Just a closer walk with thee, grant it, Jesus if you please. Daily walking close to thee, let it be, dear Lord, let it be."

The quenching of our thirst and the source of our strength comes from Jesus. When we feel weak, we just need to ask Jesus to let us have a closer walk with Him. You will discover that it is through His thirst on the cross for us that our thirst can be quenched and satisfied. He took care of thirst for the whole world, so that our thirst could be satisfied. Praise our God.

There is a song that says, "I got a river of life flowing out of me, makes the lame to walk and the blind to see. Opens prison doors, sets the captives free. I've got a river of life flowing out of me. Spring up, oh well, down in my soul. Spring up, oh well, and make me whole. Spring up, oh well, and give to me that life abundantly...." If we go to Jesus' well on a daily basis, then we will not search the world to quench our thirst. Even after we are saved, He wants us to drink by worshipping and honoring Him.

You can quench your thirst with abundant life, and you can have it today, tomorrow and forever!

Lessons On Being Thirsty

1. What is the power of denial, as witnessed through what Jesus said and refrained from doing on the cross?

2. How does Jesus' statement "I thirst" line up with His destiny?

3. How is your destiny attached to that of Jesus?

4. Jesus' physical suffering created a thirst for His physical deliverance. How does this reality affect your understanding of Jesus' sensitivity to your cries for help and deliverance? (Consider how God's word in Heb. 4:14-16 depicts Jesus as one who can identify and sympathize with us.)

5. How did Jesus also manifest His thirst for the salvation of the world?

6. What are you thirsty for that this world cannot supply? (Consider the following Scriptures: Ps. 42:1-2a; Isa. 55:1-3; Mt. 5:6; Jn. 4:13-14; Jn. 7:37-38)

Chapter Six: A Lesson on Being Triumphant

Let us go on to the sixth statement Jesus made from the cross. We traditionally call this "The Words of Triumph." Jesus said, "It is finished." When we review the previous words He has spoken, this statement is ambiguous.

First, He said," Father forgive them, for they know not what they do." That seems pretty clear. Next, He acknowledges and remembers the thief saying, "This day shalt thou be with Me in paradise." That is also clear. His third statement is "Woman, behold thy son." Then, speaking to John, he says, "Son, behold thy mother." That is also pretty clear. In His fourth statement, He cries, "My God, why hast thou forsaken me?" We know what He meant by that. The fifth time He spoke, He was fulfilling scripture, saying, "I am thirsty."

Now He says, "It is finished." The ambiguity comes from the word "it," for there is no contextual reference to what this "it" may be. There is no surrounding text that clarifies what "it" is.

So what does He mean when He says, "It is finished?" In order to understand Him, we need to make sure that we know why Jesus came from heaven to earth. We need to understand His purpose, and the focus of His pilgrimage to terra firma. We need to understand why He took off His robe of glory and traveled through 42 generations, why He dwelt amongst us, and why He walked in Galilee and Nazareth.

There are four meanings to the statement, "It is finished."

The first meaning lies in the fact that He had suffered sufficiently. He had watched us from the portals of glory as we tried futilely to atone for our own sins. He suffered as He continuously saw us crumbling under the weight of sin and the law. Even when He came to earth as a child, He suffered. Misunderstood by His parents, rejected by His own people, harshly criticized by the Pharisees, and deserted by His own disciples, Jesus *suffered*. He suffered as He was run out of town and almost killed after performing a miracle. He suffered as He was denied by Peter and betrayed by Judas. Jesus continually suffered while here on earth.

Now on the cross, He suffered for a crime that He did not commit. He was an innocent man taking the place of guilty men and women. He offered His own body as a sacrifice for the atonement of our sins. He hung on the cross at the pinnacle of human suffering just so that we could have the right to the tree of life.

He suffered on the cross. They whipped Him with bone and metal that tore and ripped His flesh. His hands bore the marks of stakes that were nailed through them. He wore a prickly crown of thorns, not a crown befitting the King of Kings. Remember His agony as His blood gushed out of His side after being pierced with a sword.

He suffered all of this on the cross - the reviling of the thieves, the gambling of His garments by those soldiers, and the spitting in His face. And as He hung there, He knew that most of the people had betrayed Him when He needed them most. And when all was completed, Jesus said, "It is finished." In other words, His suffering was over. When Jesus said, " I thirst," He was summoning death to come. As the Lord of life and death, death had to wait until Jesus had finished suffering for us and was ready for death to come. At that point, He was able to say, "It is finished."

But then there is a second thing to mention. He had satisfied the scriptures. His birth was prophesied in Isaiah 9, with Isaiah's prophesy about the forthcoming Messiah. "And the government shall be upon His shoulders. And we shall call Him Mighty God, Prince of Peace, and Everlasting Father."

God prophesied through the writings of Moses as He recorded the first human activity in the world. After Adam sinned and transgressed the law of God in Genesis 3:15, God administered His curses. But He also let them know that as the serpent had bruised the heel of the first Adam, the second Adam (Jesus Christ) would take the same heel and bruise the serpent's head.

His life was prophesied in the scriptures. In Matthew 2:15, it says that Jesus was taken by His mother and Joseph into Egypt so that the scripture might be fulfilled. "Out of Egypt have I called my Son." In Matthew 2:23, it said that He would be the one who would live in Nazareth; therefore, He was called a Nazarene. The Bible speaks of His birth and His life, but it also foretells His death. In Isaiah 53 it says: "He was wounded for our transgressions, bruised for our iniquities, the chastisement of our peace was upon Him and with His stripes we are healed." Each word from the cross was uttered to satisfy the Scriptures. In Psalm 34:20, we learn that not one bone would be broken in His body, but all else would happen because He had to satisfy the Scriptures.

So, the first thing that "it" refers to is His suffering. His suffering is finished.

The second meaning behind "it" is the fulfillment of the scriptures. He had to remain aligned with the word of God.

The third thing that He did was secure our salvation! He secured it for all time. He did not have to die anymore. He did not have to suffer anymore. He only had to declare that it was done, give up the ghost and allow our salvation to be passed down unto us.

His death on the cross is so significant. In dying, He secured our salvation. Matthew 28 says: "He became a ransom for us all." Because of our sins and disobedience, there was a ransom on all of humanity. Jesus satisfied that ransom note. Not only did He become a ransom and secure our salvation, but He also reconciled

God and man. Romans 5:10-11 talks about how He reconciled us unto God. In other words, He brought us back and restored us to the fellowship we once had with Him in Adam. This bond, broken by Adam, was restored by the second Adam, who is Jesus the Christ. Think about the glory of that! He secured our salvation by becoming a ransom, a reconciler, and a substitute for us. Every one of us should have been on the cross. We had a debt that we could not pay. Therefore, Jesus had to pay it for us.

But then there's another thing that He did in securing our salvation. Not only did He become a ransom, a reconciler and also a substitute, but He also became what the King James Version calls propitiation. Read I John 2:2 and John 4:10 and you will discover that Jesus became a propitiation for us, which means that He became a covering. He made sure we received God's mercy. Mercy prevents us from receiving what we really deserve. By hanging on the cross, He prevented us from receiving what we actually deserved. He spared us, which was something that we could not do ourselves. But wait; there is a fourth and final thing Jesus did. When Jesus said, "It is finished," He said it in triumph! Go back to

Genesis 3:15. You will find that "it" refers to the fact that He struck a deadly blow to Satan.

As He uttered the words, "It is finished," He wanted the world to know that we need not worry about the devil as our enemy. While on that cross, Jesus took that same heel and bruised the head of the devil. Injured, the devil is on his way to death, where God is going to banish him forever. Knowing that he can never win a battle against Jesus, the devil tries to raise hell and havoc in our lives. While he cannot get Jesus, he still tries to attack us. But greater is He that is in us than he that is in the world! If you want to be triumphant, then you need to stick with Jesus. Through His triumph, we are triumphant. If you want a lesson on being triumphant, then come to know Jesus Christ as your personal Lord and Savior, and watch the triumph that you'll experience in your own life! When Jesus said, "It is finished," He basically said, "I've done all that I came to do. I've suffered sufficiently, I have made sure that I've satisfied the scriptures, and I've secured their salvation. I have struck a deadly blow to Satan; now I can give up the ghost. I can breathe my last breath. Since it is finished, I now can place my life in the hands of my God."

It had been a long and exhausting night. But at last, it was finished. The ordeal had been extremely painful. But at last, it was finished. The plan of Salvation, by grace, had been a long time coming. But at last, it was finished. The battle had been intense and the victory took some time. But finally, it was finished. The sacrifice to atone for sin for the entire world was now complete. The many prophecies foretelling this day and hour had finally been fulfilled, and Jesus was able to go out triumphantly. For at last, it was finished.

Because it is finished, because salvation has been secured, and because He satisfied the scriptures we can sing the hymn written by William Cowperi years ago, *"There is a fountain filled with blood drawn from Emmanuel's veins; And sinners plunged beneath that flood lose all their guilty stains..."* Because it is finished, sinners can plunge beneath the flood and lose the stain of their guilt. That is why we can look at the devil and say, "In the name of Jesus, we have victory!" for He shed His blood, just for us.

Jesus is the one who suffered. Jesus is the one who satisfied the scriptures. Jesus is the one who secured our salvation. Jesus is the one who beat the devil. In His name, we have victory. So we can sing, "Victory is mine!" You may be going through rough things right now. Even Jesus had to go through pain and suffering. But when it was all over, He came out triumphant. He went in bloody. He went in ugly. He suffered beyond what we can comprehend, but when He got through, He said, "It is finished." He came out whiter than snow. So whatever you are going through, hang in there.

You may have to suffer, but He has already secured your salvation. Tell the devil he is a liar! He has no victory. He has no place in your marriage. He has no place, in your body. He has no place in your children. He has no place on your job, because Jesus paid it all. We owe Him everything. Sin left a crimson stain, but Jesus washed it, and it is whiter than snow.

It is finished…today.

Jesus did not say it might be finished *someday*. He said that it is finished right here and now. You can be broken or in turmoil over something, but remember, God's work has already been finished. You might be worrying about your health, a family member or your past, but remember: God's work is finished. Thank God for *this* day!

Now, you must also act like and believe that it is finished. The wall may still be standing, but you must behave like it has crumbled to the ground. You still might be experiencing problems in a relationship, but you must claim that it has been mended. If we allow the One who is the greatest example of triumph to be triumphant in our hearts, then we can experience triumph in our lives! He did not die for you to be the tail. He died for you to be the head. He did not die for you to be down; He died for you to be up. He did not die just so that you could have life, but He died that you might have it more abundantly.

"It is finished," means that it never has to be repeated. Once you accept Jesus Christ as your personal Lord and Savior, His salvation is so complete, that when He saves you, you never need to be saved again. When He saves you, none of your wrong doings can annul or reverse your salvation. You know why? You did not *earn* your salvation, so you cannot lose it. The Bible says that it is by grace through faith that we are saved, not because of anything we can do ourselves. It is God's gift to us, not the works of any man, woman, boy or girl. It is finished!

God wants to finish some things in your life. Now, that does not mean that everything is going to instantaneously be made right. It does mean, however, that once you place yourself and your circumstances in His hands, then you *are* triumphant. Now, you may have to wait for the process to move into full fruition, but remember this: Jesus had to suffer. He had to stay on the cross until it was all done. If you want a personal relationship with God, through Jesus Christ, all you have to say is that you believe that Jesus Christ is the Son of God that He died on the cross for your sins, and God raised Him from the dead.

As the Bible says, you will be saved. You do not have to foam at the mouth or speak in unknown tongues. You do not have to flip over any church pews. All you have to do is just say what you believe in your heart.

If you are already a Christian, but do not feel that you have been as triumphant as you could be, make Christ number one in your life. Go out and find membership with fellow believers in our Lord and Savior. Find a church that is filled with the love of God.

If you have strayed away or backslidden, but you want to come back, restore fellowship with God, then allow Him to be in control.

Jesus endured the cruelty of the cross for some six hours. Having summoned death via his sixth utterance from the cross, "It is finished," Jesus was ready for his departure.

Lessons On Being Triumphant

1. "It is finished," refers to four things that Jesus accomplished through His death. What are they?

2. Could Jesus have been completely triumphant without having accomplished all four things? Why or why not?

3. How does Jesus, through His death on the cross, provide us with assurance of triumph in our lives, despite persecution and pain? (Jn. 16:33; Rom. 8:28, 37)

4. Jesus' suffering and sacrifice was spiritually redemptive for all who believe in Him. Has your suffering and sacrifice ever been spiritually or temporally redemptive/beneficial for someone else?

5. Despite terror and tragedy, list the triumphs that you have experienced in your life because of Jesus Christ. How did your personal relationship with Jesus cause you to triumph? (2 Cor. 4:7-12)

6. How has Jesus' finished work on the cross allowed you to triumph over the weight and burden of sin in your life, both in terms of the ultimate penalty for sin and your daily struggle with sin? (2 Cor. 5:17-21; Col. 1:13-14; Col. 2:13-15; Hebrews 9:28)

Chapter Seven: A Lesson On Being In His Hands

Before he surrendered himself into the temporary custody of death, Jesus, our dying Savior, would teach us a final lesson from the cross. In His last words, Jesus mouthed for us the importance and necessity of being in God's hands. He said, "Father, into THY Hands, I commend my Spirit."

In Greek (the original language of the New Testament), "commend" means to "deposit with another, to give another charge, to be placed in another's custody, to entrust another with something precious." Therefore, Jesus, in his death, provides us with a lesson on giving God charge over our lives. It is a lesson about entrusting God with our lives and putting ourselves in His hands.

Too many people place parts of their lives in God's hands, but not their entire *lives* in His hands. When we give God our problems, but not our lives, we end up settling for a temporary fix when God wants to grant us permanent deliverance. If you simply give God your problems, but never your life, the most you will ever receive is a fixed problem. Your life might still be a mess!

In His death, Jesus teaches us that it was not just His suffering that He commended to God. He placed His life into the hands of Almighty God, His Father. Although she was near the cross, Jesus did not even attempt to place His life in the hands of Mary, His mother. He never attempted to place His life in the hands of John, His beloved disciple and friend. Instead, Jesus placed His life in the hands of His Father.

There is something about our Heavenly Father's hands that evokes and invokes trust. In His hands, we are able to live by faith, when we would otherwise walk by sight. Like Joshua, we can step into something like the Jordan River at flood time, and yet know we will be alright because we are in the Father's hands.

On the day He beckoned Peter to walk out on the water, there was something about Jesus' hands. Peter walked out with confidence, knowing that when he began to sink, as long as he was lifted in Jesus' hands (which were an earthly manifestation of the Father's hands), he would not be in any danger.

From birth to death, Jesus put His life in the Father's hands. Despite all that Jesus experienced, He was able to die with a sense of contentment and completion. His life was in the Father's hands. Regardless of what occurred during His daily walk, He lived victoriously because His life was in the Father's hands.

If we place our lives in the Father's hands, then we will experience something that too many have died without knowing: a sense of contentment and completion. The very moment that we place our lives in the Father's hands, we have both.

Once we accept the gift of living in God's hands, we will live forever in the midst of calm and tranquility. No matter what happens, we will know that ultimately, everything will be alright. There are no true, eternal problems and no unending storms on the horizon.

Trying to be independent and self-sufficient leaves you in an incredibly vulnerable position. That same mentality will turn around and attack and plague you if your life is not in His hands. All too often, human beings have a tendency to believe that all is handled and under control when things are going smoothly. And, if we are not careful, we will applaud our own merits instead of thanking God for our peace and calm. Eventually, the calm can coax us into thinking that we do not need God because nothing seems to be wrong. Ironically, we are our most vulnerable when we believe that things are calm because of our own doing. When things are going well, we even stop seeking the Lord and honoring Him as our source and supply. Most of us *play* in the calm and *pray* in the storm. I think we better reverse that!

We need to learn how to pray in the calm so that we can play in the storm. Pray when things are smooth, and pray when things are rough. Make sure your life is in His hands *at all times.*

Chaos, confusion and disorder will come, but do not let it throw you. Put yourself in His hands. Chaos can challenge our emotional stability and even rock our faith. It may even make us wonder whether God is still on the throne or answers prayers. We cry out, but is seems as if there is no reply. However, as promised in Isaiah 3:26, if we give God charge over our lives and keep our minds on Him, then He will keep us in perfect peace. Peace stops chaos in its tracks. Peace is what we need in the midst of a storm. God has the power to say, "Peace! Be still," and end the storm.

You must be in His hands. Another writer put it this way:

Does the path seem rough and steep? Leave it to God.
Do you sow but fail to reap?
Leave it to God.
Do you yield to him your human will?
Listen humbly and just be still,
Love divine your mind can fill,
Leave it to God.
Is your life an uphill fight?
Leave it to God.
Do you struggle for the right?
Leave it to God.
Though the way may be dreary and long,
Sorrow will give place to song,

Good must triumph over wrong,
Leave it to God.
If in doubt just what to do,
Leave it to God.
He will make it plain to you,
Leave it to God.
Serve him faithfully today,
He will guide you all the way,
Simply trust, watch, and pray,
Leave it to God.

If your life is in His hands, then you can sleep even though chaos is around you. Knowing that you have a God who does not sleep allows you to lie down, rest and have peace of mind.

Not only must we be in His hands in the calm and chaos, but we must also be in His hands amidst calamity. Calamity differs from chaos; it is a major loss or disaster. While I hope that calamity never afflicts you, none of us is exempt.

And if and when calamity comes, our lives need to be in His hands. If your life is not in His hands, then you might become angry with God. You might forget the fact that He is Sovereign. You may forget the fact that although God does not cause everything, He does allow some things. You may not understand why He is allowing it, but if your life is in His hands, you will know as Paul did: "Know that all things work together for the good of them who love the Lord and are called according to His purpose." It may not look good to you at the time, but you can be assured that God is going to work it out to be good for you in the end.

Sometimes inexplicably, calamity strikes. You are unable to explain it and you did not see it coming. Even now, some of you are experiencing disaster and loss. One minute your life was fine, and now it seems to have been ground into the earth. Now, more than ever, you have to make sure that your life is in His hands.

While God is always strong, there are times that we may feel weak. However, we do not have to be self-critical for not being strong all of the time. In fact, the devil will make you believe that there is something wrong with you for being weak in the midst of calamity. However, there are some things in this life, no matter how much you pray, fast, and read the word, that will be too heavy for you to bear.

In those times, it is important to remember that your life is in His hands. Paul knew that his life was in God's hands. Paul went to God and said, "Lord, I have this thorn in the flesh, I have this problem and I can't get rid of it." He asked God for help three times. God said, "No, Paul, My grace is sufficient for thee. For My strength is made perfect in your weakness."

James H. McConkey put it this way: "Don't try to be strong, just be still."

Watson Tainer was so feeble in the closing months of his life that he wrote a dear friend, "I am so weak. I cannot work. I cannot read my Bible. I cannot even pray. I can only lie still in God's arms like a little child and trust." This wondrous man of God, with all of his spiritual power, came to a place of physical suffering and weakness where he could only lie still and trust. But you know that is all that God asks of you and me. When you grow faint in the fierce fires of affliction, do not try to be strong, just be still, for your life is in His hands. And, if you are still long enough, then you will see the foundation of the Lord in your life.

So, whether its calm, chaos, or calamity we are experiencing, we should place our lives in our Father's hands. Jesus, in His death as in His life, trusted God to have His life in His hands.

God's hands are pure hands. His hands are gentle, caressing, and they can mold us. He is the potter and we are the clay. His hands are creating hands. In six days, He made the world! His hands are strong and mighty. His hands are trustworthy and nurturing. His hands are tender and secure. His hands are competent. His hands are healing!

Jesus was a healer, but His healing power came from the hands of the Father. He can and will deliver you from any circumstance. If you let Him, He will work wonders and miracles in your life. He can lay His healing hands on you and baffle the doctor's mind. He can lay His redemptive hands on you and cause the judge to reverse his own decision. He is a miracle worker! His hands give life. His hands are wise. His hands are powerful. His hands are anointed. His hands are safe. No matter the problem, issues, situation or circumstance, whatever you are going through, put it *all* in His hands. He can handle it.

But do not stop at just giving Him your *circumstances*; do not stop at just giving Him your trouble, your future, your illness, your debt or your confusion. Do not just give Him your health or your problems. Make sure you put your *life* in His hands. He will guide you. He will keep you. He will direct you. He will watch over you. He will make ways for you.

Be a bold, compassionate Christian. Find somebody else in the world who is suffering and say, "I don't know what you're going through, and I don't know what you're dealing with. What I do know is if you put it in His hands, everything will be alright."

Put everything, not some things, in His hands.

When you put your whole life in His hands, everything is covered. No matter how severe it is you will conquer it and experience contentment beyond your wildest dreams. Now, let us just be still. Still. Be still. God is going to do what He is going to do. Stop moving and stay out of the way. Let Him prepare the way. Just be still and be sure *you* are entirely in His hands.

Hallelujah, God is speaking even now. Somebody needs to put his or her life in His hands. Perhaps you have been praying about situations or circumstances. You have been giving them to God, but you have not given Him *you*. Sometimes, God will not change your circumstances because He wants to change you first. If your circumstances change, but you are unchanged, then you will find yourself in a perpetual cycle of destruction. So, in the stillness of this very moment, you can decide that you are going to let Him change you. You can ask Him to make a difference in your *life*, not just your present circumstance. Whether there is calm, chaos, or calamity in your life, you do not have to be afraid ever again. Though you may not know how it will to work out, when you put your life in God's hands, peace and serenity will come. Because your life is in His hands, God is going to work it out.

Lessons On Being In His Hands

1. When you have tried to take matters into your own hands, what has the result been?

2. When and why have you been most reluctant to put yourself and your circumstances in God's hands?

3. Have you ever placed something in God's hands only to take it back? Does this tendency indicate a struggle with trust, patience and/or control?

4. What has been the result when you have completely placed things in God's hands and allowed God to handle them?

5. Write down what comes to mind when you think about God's hands. (Ps. 37:23-24; Ps. 139:7-10; Jn. 10:28-30)

6. How can you entrust more to God's hands (i.e. problems, decisions, spiritual growth and maturity, health, finances, etc.)?

Chapter Eight: A Lesson for the Hopeless

Friday must have been the worst day for Mary Magdalene, John (the beloved disciple) and the other women. After all, Friday represented the last of everything that could cause them to appreciatively applaud, submissively obey and put their faith in Jesus. Friday, you must recall, was when they heard His last utterances before His death. According to the Gospels, Jesus made seven utterances while dying on the cross. They were His last. In all likelihood, every utterance of Jesus from the cross was etched into the heads and hearts of His mother, friends and most loyal followers. When they saw Him take His last breath, it had to take their breath away. When they saw His bruised and battered body lowered from the cross and placed in a borrowed tomb, it was the last time that they could supportively follow Him. When they watched His tomb being sealed, they thought it would be the last time they would see Him. The stone that sealed the tomb also sealed their last hope and may have dismantled their belief that He was the

Messiah. Without Jesus, there was no more hope.

It appeared that Jesus was more of a man than He was a Messiah. The grave seemed to have stolen their hope and sense of victory by taking custody of Jesus' corpse. Death had won. Mark's gospel notes that while Jesus was on the cross, "the curtain in the temple was torn in two from top to bottom" (Mark. 15:38). The Apostle Paul later interpreted the symbolism of Mark's statement in Ephesians 2:14-18, suggesting that when the curtain or veil was torn, it represented Jesus' destruction of the wall or barrier between God and humanity. Consequently, humanity could have direct access to and intimacy with God through Jesus. In all probability, however, Jesus' followers felt more like the curtain had been lowered; the darkness of their souls was impenetrable. They had to feel a momentary estrangement from God, not an enhanced intimacy with Him.

Many of us have known the dark night of the soul. Many of us have had our hopes dashed. Every human being knows or will eventually learn that things do not always work out the way we would prefer. Life has a way of challenging our faith. We must confront and conquer this seeming hopelessness. As we reference our own experiences of apparent hopelessness, it should not be difficult to imagine the spiritual and emotional crisis into which Mary, John and the other women must have been thrust.

Hopelessness, after all, is the absence of confidence for a favorable outcome. Hopelessness suggests that one lacks any positive expectation. Hopelessness is the state where one no longer has a reason to believe things will improve. Hopelessness is that place of despair that incapacitates or paralyzes one's ability to see or willingness to embrace the idea of distant deliverance. Hopelessness causes one to give up on the possibility of positive change. Ultimately, hopelessness causes one to accept present reality as permanent reality. But there are some relevant questions that must be dealt with before we totally resign to an utter state of hopelessness.

The questions that we must confront can only be raised and answered objectively. Are we actually bankrupt of hope when we resign to seeming hopelessness? By what extreme deduction do we relegate ourselves and/or our situations to a state of hopelessness? Is not a dim or even indiscernible light in the distance a glimmer of hope, albeit at the extreme end of our darkness? Does hope cease to exist simply because it is hidden from our view, kept from our senses? The answer to these queries about hopelessness lies in the final lesson from our Savior.

The final lesson for our consideration is the lesson that Jesus teaches in transformational transition. In other words, Jesus teaches this lesson as He is transitioning and transforming from the dying Savior to the risen and living Savior and Lord. He uses the dark backdrop of His death and burial to shine the bright light of hope in the wake of His resurrection. Then, through the experiences of Mary Magdalene and the other women, in particular, He teaches us lessons of hope. Jesus also taught Mary, His disciples, and us a lesson of hope for the hopeless. Consider, as exemplified in Mary and the other women, the responsibilities of the hopeless.

First, we must *return* to the place where it appeared that our hopes were dashed. For Mary and the other women, they had to return to the grave where Jesus was buried. In that place, their hopelessness was sealed. At the tomb, the actuality of Jesus' fate and their hopelessness became an undeniable reality. Yet, just as they returned to face reality, you and I must as well.

Each Gospel writer notes, with each giving his own editorial highlight that Mary Magdalene and the women returned to the tomb after the Sabbath. In Matthew 27:61, Matthew notes that the women witnessed the entombment of Jesus. Therefore, they knew where Jesus was buried and were able to return to the exact location.

But can you imagine their inner emotions as they returned to the tomb? The Lord often causes us to return to a place of hopelessness, disappointment or failure so that we might experience the assurance of hope, fulfillment, success, and ultimately, the miraculous. The significance of returning to such a place is that Jesus teaches them and us that hope can be found alive in the place where we thought it died!

When they returned to the tomb they discovered hope alive. When they returned to the tomb, they found that the stone had been rolled away. When they returned to the tomb, they were not met by guards who forbade them from properly embalming Jesus' dead body. Rather, they were met by an angel who announced Jesus' resurrection to them. The angel said to the women, "Do not be afraid, for I know that you are looking for Jesus, who was crucified. He is not here; He has risen. . . " (Matthew 28:5-6a). Now that is hope alive!

Sometimes we shy away from or avoid returning to a place of lost hope. Jesus teaches us, however, that the place of lost hope is often the place where hope is restored. The place where we resigned to hopelessness is also the place where hope is renewed. On one occasion, Jesus told Peter to return to the fishing spot where he had toiled all night and caught nothing. Reluctantly, Peter returned. When he returned, however, he ended up catching so many fish that he had to solicit help to bring in all of the fish (Luke 5:4-11). The Lord will give you hope and a future (Jeremiah 29:11). Therefore, do not be afraid to return to the place where your hopes were dashed. Because of Jesus Christ, Biblical hope is called confident expectation. As long as Jesus is who He is (Hebrews 13:8), there will always be a glimmer of hope. Do not give up on Jesus.

Second, we must *remember* what Jesus said. The angel told the women that Jesus had risen "...just as He said" (Matthew 28:6a). This suggests that the women had already heard Jesus prophesy not only His death, but also His resurrection (John 10:17-18). Therefore, they should not have allowed themselves to languish in the dungeon of despair or the house of hopelessness. Moreover, they were not the only ones to have heard Jesus' prophetic proclamations.

Because of Jesus' prophetic proclamations, the guards who were stationed outside the place of Jesus' entombment were assigned to duty. The chief priests and Pharisees requested extra security because they remembered what Jesus said. "Sir," they said, "we remember that while He was still alive, that deceiver said, 'After three days, I will rise again.' So give the order for the tomb to be made secure until the third day (Matthew. 27:63-64a). They remembered Jesus' words and wanted to assure themselves that He would not rise from the dead. They wanted to secure their hopes that Jesus would not do what He said.

Conversely, grief and bewilderment must have gripped the women and Jesus' disciples to the point that they temporarily forgot what He taught and preached throughout His ministry. Apparently, the women and Jesus' disciples had no expectations that Jesus was going to do what He said He would do. Hence, the women rose early that morning after the Sabbath intending only to embalm Jesus' dead body.

How many times do we fail to remember what the Lord has said He will do? How easy it is for us to have a case of scriptural amnesia in the face of seeming hopelessness? Even when attending worship services, Bible studies, revivals, conferences, workshops and the like, hopelessness causes us to accept our present reality as permanent reality. My friends, no one's word should be able to make us discard, disregard or doubt the word of our Savior and Lord. His word is supreme, superior, superlative, and supernatural. If the Lord said it, you can count on it.

Whenever you face seemingly hopeless situations, remember His word. There is hope in His word (Psalms 46:1). There is salvation in His word (Romans 10:9-13). There is strength in His word (Isaiah 40:31). There is peace in His word (Philippians 4:6-7). There is assurance in His word (Matthew 28:20b; Luke 1:37). There is wisdom in His word (James 1:5). There is confidence in His word (1 John 5:14-15). There is life in His word (John 10:10; 14:6a). There is resurrection in His word (John 10:17-18; 11:25-26). Remember what Jesus said! Therein lies your hope.

Third, *rejoice* over what the risen Savior has done. So the women hurried away from the tomb, afraid yet filled with joy, and ran to tell the disciples (Matthew 28:8). What did Jesus do to restore their hope and fill their hearts with joy?

Firstly, He rose from the dead just as he said. Secondly, He transformed hopelessness into hope through his resurrection. Thirdly, He changed the women's story from one of gloom to one of glory. Fourthly, He filled their bankrupt hearts with a surplus of joy and existential hope for the future.

But what has He done to restore your hope and fill your heart with joy? Dear friends, Jesus can and will restore your hope and fill your heart with joy. I assure you that when no one else can, Jesus can create a transforming transition in your circumstances that will turn your midnight into day. When no one else can, Jesus can make light shine in the most intense darkness of your human experience. When no one else can, Jesus can teach a lesson to the hopeless that leaves them hopeful. Jesus can do what no other power can do.

In 2003, the church that I pastored was bursting at the seams. The church had exceeded its capacity in every area: worship space, parking space, educational space and administrative space. The church grew from two to three morning worship services. The church was landlocked. In a nutshell, we needed to relocate.

I began to seek God's will and search for land on which to build. We found approximately 46 acres and initiated the process of securing the land (with the city's approval). If you know anything about land and construction, not to mention negotiating contracts, the process is usually lengthy. Therefore, we were led to continue the process, but seek a viable alternative.

We prayed and investigated many options. At last, a 48,000-square foot building became available. It would require significant renovations to make it meet our needs, but it seemed to be God's will. We would be able to expand our worship seating capacity from less than 400 to just over 1,000. Our classroom space could increase from six classrooms to 20 multipurpose rooms. Our administrative capacity would increase from four offices to a space that could accommodate 14 staff persons. Parking would increase from under 100 to over 300 parking spaces, with additional parking access and much more. It was an ideal situation to sustain and increase our growth momentum.

After several months of negotiations with the building's owners, they walked away from the table without any rhyme or reason. We were negotiating for a lease with a purchase option. Things were seemingly going well when the bottom fell out of the deal. Needless to say, even as a pastor, I saw our hopes dashed. What would or could we do? As the "new" pastor, my leadership credibility was at stake. I could be viewed as an inept leader who could not spiritually discern the will of God with clarity. The situation seemed hopeless.

We could not stay where we were without significantly losing momentum and declining. As things stood, some people would never enter the church grounds on Sundays. Discouraged, disappointed and unable to find parking within reasonable walking distance, they would simply leave. I prayed. The leadership prayed. Nothing! It seemed that hope was on holiday. But then, after several months of consternation, there was a phone call.

Out of the clear blue and without any communication since walking away from the table, we received a call from the senior partner of the owner's group. He said, "Sir, if you're still interested, I believe that I have a deal this time that you won't be able to refuse." In the span of three weeks, the Lord gave us what it took nine months to lose! The Lord caused us to return to the place where our hopes were dashed. The Lord caused me to remember what He said to me, "it's yours." When the documents for the building were signed with a mortgage rather than the former lease, the Lord said to me, "it's what you asked me for." I rejoiced with the people of God as I shared with them what the Lord had done. He did what he said and more. As I write, our church rejoices over almost two years of being in our new facility.

The final lesson from our dying Savior, who is now our risen Savior, is that as long as He is who He is, there is hope. *I am He that liveth, and was dead; and, behold, I am alive for evermore, Amen; and have the keys of hell and death* (Revelation1:18, KJV). Believe and expect the Lord to do the impossible in your life and circumstances. Never give up on Jesus. In Jesus and Him alone there is hope!

Lessons on Hope

1. Is your definition of hope consistent with the biblical understanding of hope presented in this chapter? If so, how? If not, how does your definition differ?

2. Have you ever felt hopeless? Can you identify with Mary Magdalene, the disciples and the other women in their hopelessness? If so, describe and discuss one of your experiences of hopelessness.

3. How did your experience of disappointment or devastation affect the level or existence of your expectations?

4. Was your hope ever restored? If so, is there a direct relationship between your relationship in Jesus and your transformational transition from hopelessness to hopefulness? If not, how are you managing your faith and emotions in light of your disappointing experience?

5. How have you learned to hold onto your hope amidst seemingly hopeless circumstances?

6. How have your experiences with seeming hopelessness equipped you to handle the possibility of hopelessness in the future?

Epilogue

Chances are that most of you, as readers of this book, have read and heard these lessons before. The goal of this book was not to introduce its readers to anything new. Rather, this book was written to elevate our appreciation and application of these living lessons in light of the context of death out of which they emerge.

In His death and resurrection, our dying Savior and risen Lord modeled lessons of incalculable practical worth. From forgiveness and compassion, to the family and on feeling forsaken, Jesus taught His final lessons in an indelible manner. From being thirsty and triumphant to being in the Father's hands and reminding us that even hope that is dead is not done, Jesus taught lessons that time will not erode. Lessons, however, are only as good as the application of those who learn them.

The challenge of every believer is to live out the lessons of our Savior and Lord. It is His will that we be doers of the word, not just hearers (James 1:22). Therefore, each of us must be intentional about fully comprehending and faithfully applying the last lessons of our Savior and Lord. My prayer is that the lessons Jesus taught through His death will be manifested in you and me. In turn, all people will know that we are His disciples.

Learn, teach, and live these lessons taught by our Savior and Lord, Jesus the Christ.